Arabic & Persian Poems

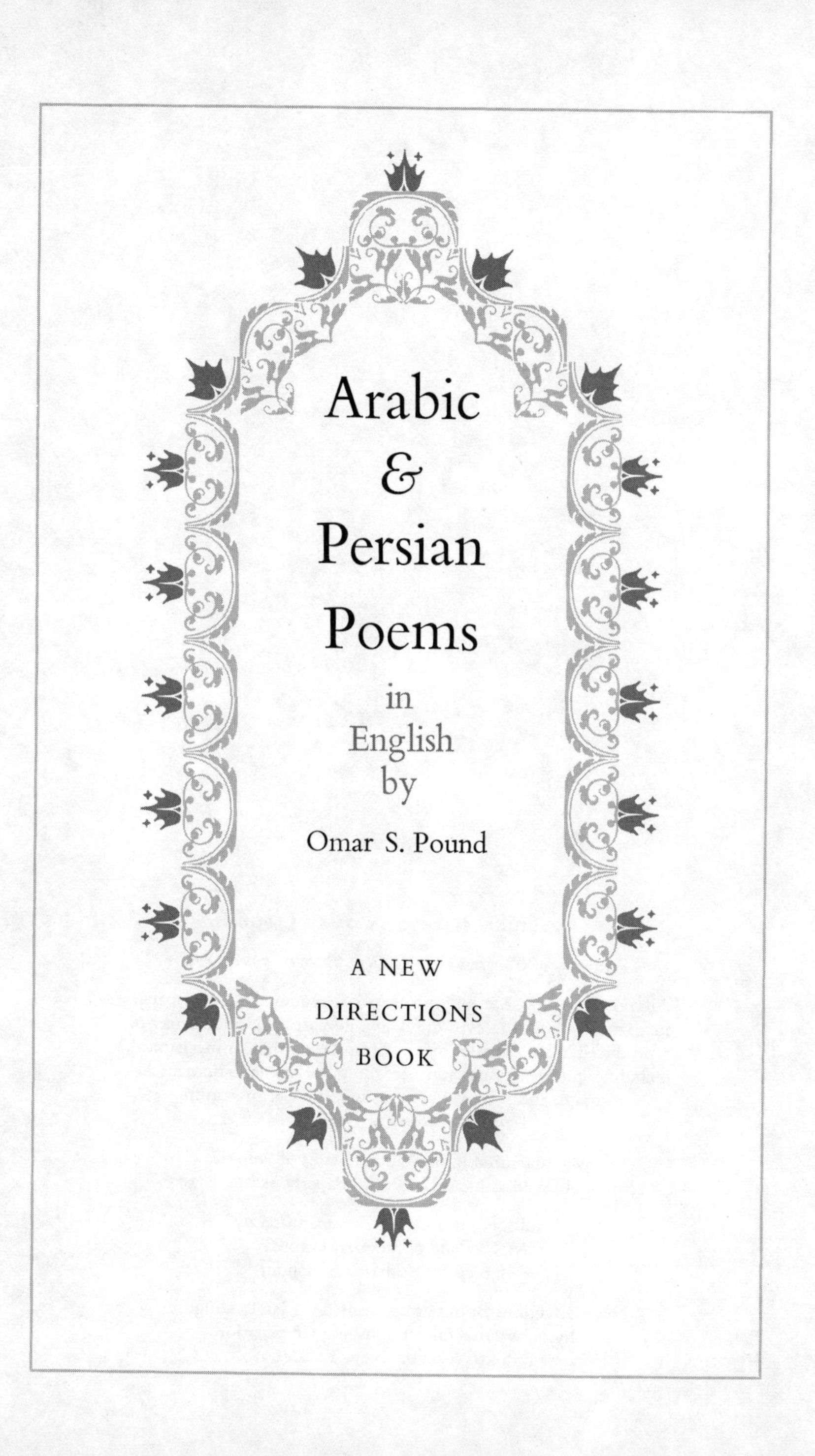

Arabic & Persian Poems

in English by

Omar S. Pound

A NEW DIRECTIONS BOOK

Library of Congress Catalog Card Number: 79–122106

Manufactured in the United States of America
First published as New Directions Paperbook 305 in 1970

Published simultaneously in Canada by
McClelland & Stewart, Limited
Designed by Roderick Stinehour

New Directions Books are published for James Laughlin
by New Directions Publishing Corporation
333 Sixth Avenue, New York 10014

Contents

Foreword by Basil Bunting 11

Introduction 12

Introduction to Arabic Poetry 13

Introduction to Persian Poetry 23

Arabic

Al-Abbas ibn al-Ahnaf *died 808?*
Love 43

Abid ibn al-Abras *fl. 500–550*
An Arab Chieftain to His Young Wife 32
Lament for an Arab Encampment 31

Abu Dhu'ayb al-Hudhali *died 649?*
Lament for Five Sons Lost in a Plague 35

Abu Dulama *died 776/7?*
Behold My Mother 40
Traders in Beauty and Delight 41

Abu Ishaq al-Ilbiri *died 1067*
Granada (1000 A.D.) 51

Abu Nuwas *747?–815?*
The Rake 42

Dhu'l-Rumma *696?–735/6?*
Of All Garments 38

Al-Hutay'a *600?–661/2?*
It Is New 34

Ibn Hazm al-Andalusi *994–1064*
Twice Times Then Is Now 50

Ibn al-Rumi *836–896*
Slow Giving 44
The Compromise 45
The Weighing-In 44
To a Hunchback (attributed) 45

Al-Ifriqi al-Mutayyam *fl. 975*
My Wife Complains I Pray No More 48

Jamíl *660?–701*
Salsabíl 36

Al-Khansa' *590?–644?*
Lament for a Brother 33

Kuthaiyir *663?–723?*
At Her Grave 38

Al-Lajjam al-Harrani *fl. 960*
His Banquets Cure Most Ills 47

Mutanabbi *915–965*
Shame Kept My Tears Away 46

Muzahim al-Uqaili *fl. 700*
The Earth Outside 39

Al-Tirimmah *660?–725?*
In the Heart of the Desert 37
Lord of the Throne 37

Unknown *9th century?*
Waves 49

Persian

Anvari *1126?–1189/90?*
Hors de Combat 59

Jalal al-din Rumi *1207–1273*
Quatrain 65

Jamal Isfahani *died 1192*
White Hairs 64

Kemal Khojandi *died 1401?*
One Final Fling 66

Minuchihri *died 1041?*
Demon in Paradise 57
I Send You My Verses 57
Recantation 56

Nizami Arudi *fl. 1110*
Calling the Doctor (1000 A.D.) 60

Rashidi Samarqandi *fl. 1100*
Complaint to a Court Poet 58

Rudaki *870?–940/1*
Quatrain 55
Young or Old We Die 55

Biographical Notes 67

Bibliographical Note 78

For Elizabeth

Lo! Man was created anxious.
Qur'an, lxx, verse 19.

Foreword

Persian poetry has suffered badly, Arabic rather less, from neoplatonic dons determined to find an arbitrary mysticism in everything. You would think there was nothing else in Moslem poetry than nightingales which are not birds, roses which are not flowers, and pretty boys who are God in disguise. An anthology of English verse selected exclusively from George Herbert, Charles Wesley, and Father Hopkins, plus "Lead, kindly light" and "The Hound of Heaven," would be as representative as the usual samples of Persian poetry. Fitzgerald's Khayyam is the only serious exception.

There are difficulties in the way of a more satisfactory account of Persian poetry. Hafez, for instance, depends almost entirely on his mastery of sound and literary allusion, neither translatable. Minuchihri's enormous vigor and variety expresses itself often in patterns as intricate as those of a Persian carpet. Even dons are put off by the vast size of Sa'di's *Divan*, and fail to find the key poems. Much the same may be said of Arabic (in spite of Pococke's Latin versions).

There is at least as much variety in either of these literatures as in any European tongue. Fitzgerald illuminated one small corner. Now Omar Pound, selecting just the lines which match his own urbane, ironic manner, flashes a momentary light on many poets, tracing another hue in the web.

Sooner or later we must absorb Islam if our own culture is not to die of anemia. It will not be done by futile attempts to trace Maulavi symbols back to Plotinus or by reproducing in bad English verse the platitudes common to poetry everywhere. Omar Pound has detected something that Moslem poetry has in common with some of ours. He makes it credible. He makes it a pleasure. By such steps, though they may be short and few, we can at least begin our Hajj.

Basil Bunting

In presenting these examples I use only those that seem to add something fresh to English poetry. I use a few lines from one poem, a restatement of a point of view in another, a synthesis of two poems by the same author elsewhere. Occasionally I include the personal and historical circumstances of the original in the restatement, and unhesitatingly I substitute Western literary and social allusions to parallel Arabic and Persian ones—all to avoid the distraction of footnotes.

My aim: a readable poem and a rediscovery.

Omar S. Pound

Arabic Poetry

500 – 1200 A.D.

Arabic is concise and precise, and not the flowery language it is often supposed to be. The Arab prides himself on using the *mot juste,* and in ancient times many an Arab scholar is reported to have traveled great distances to find out the exact meaning of a rare word used by an obscure Bedouin tribe. Often we read of guests from far-off lands being closely cross-examined on the use and meaning of a particular word found only in the guest's tribe.

Arabic is a semitic language based on a highly developed, almost mathematical, system of triliteral roots, in which three consonants are juggled and transposed in various precise patterns to form verbs, nouns, dual forms, etc. In poetry this gives great concision in the number of syllables used, while creating an inevitable pattern of complex internal rhymes and cross-rhythms which have become an essential part of the poetry. This inherent quality of the Arabic language has also produced much rhymed prose and prose-poetry—nothing new to readers of Arabic. *Finnegans Wake* might readily have been written in Arabic. Such a style is very much part of their literary tradition.

The earliest known Arabic forms are names that occur in Assyrian records of the eighth century B.C., but the oldest texts (wall inscriptions) are from the Sinai peninsula and dated about the third century A.D. Arabic script is said to have come into use first around Hira (near Kufa in modern Iraq), a center for Bedouin poets where a substantial poetic tradition flourished in pre-Islamic times.

Arabic poetry existed long before the first written records we have—writing materials were scarce and expensive, and literacy extremely rare. It only survived in the memories of men, usually as history in the tribal traditions, but the technical complexities of the earliest known poems are so highly developed that one can assume poets had been composing and reciting their verses for several centuries previously. Form and style do not spring forth fully armed without generations or even centuries of growth. Furthermore, traces of dialect occur so rarely in these poems that one supposes that some form of "standard" Arabic was generally accepted and understood, which implies a long previous existence, considerable communication, and a common poetic diction.

There is no record of pre-Islamic poetry being written down much before 700 A.D. In fact, the earliest poems were probably not taken down until two or even three hundred years after being composed and sung—which accounts for extreme textual variations. Some scholars, including a distinguished Egyptian one, have argued that philologists of a later period forged most of the pre-Islamic poetry, but this contention has in general been satisfactorily refuted. It was chiefly in the eighth century A.D. that Arab lexicographers and philologists, realizing that the pagan poetry was being lost, made great efforts to collect and collate what had survived orally as part of each tribal tradition. They did this by searching out the *rawi*, the professional reciters and memorizers of poetry, many of whom had learned poems composed two hundred years earlier. The first anthologists used these *rawi* as primary sources, and rightly so. This revival of interest in the pagan poetry contrasts with the views of Muhammad's contemporaries who had soon completely lost interest in *jahiliya* poetry, i.e. poetry from the "days of ignorance." It was considered unbecoming, impious, and impolitic for those upholding the new faith of Islam, so they shunned it deliberately. We owe what we know of the early poetry to these later scholars, and although our knowledge is still patchy we can assemble clues, particularly to the growth of the qasida, a form used in all periods, and one which has greatly influenced non-Arab Muslim poetry, especially in Persian, Urdu, and Turkish.

The qasida is one of the oldest known forms in Arabic. The word is derived from the Arabic root *QaSaDa*, meaning "to aim," "go forward," i.e. a poem "with a purpose." Scholars are still uncertain how the qasida originated, but it seems to have grown from the *qit'a*, "fragment," a simple poem about 7–12 lines long on a single theme. By about 500 A.D. poets appear to have strung these fragments together to form the qasida, which may have evolved from their chanting and reciting these fragments and expanding them spontaneously for their listeners. Each poet would have developed individual tricks and habits to edge himself easily from one subject to the other without undue abruptness for his audience, and, over the years, this dynamic growth would have become somewhat standardized, with favorite topics molding the form to suit Bedouin taste. The form is strict enough to focus and accommodate the emotions without stifling them.

The qasida has three essential parts: (a) a visit to an abandoned encampment looking for the girl the poet loves, and then lamenting her departure; (b) the poet's love-journey to find her, which includes descriptions of desert flora and fauna, a sandstorm or desert flood, a herd of wild ass (onagers), and a short eulogy on his camel who shares the burden of the search; and (c) the final section, the "aim" and "purpose" of the poem: eulogy on a wealthy or friendly neighbor or tribe, often referring to the poet's own praiseworthy ancestry—all aimed at claiming a generous reward for the poem, or threatening poetic attack if generosity did not live up to the poet's hopes. This final section, often filled with scurrilous abuse and invective (*hija'*, inadequately translated "satire"), becomes denigrating psychological warfare against real or potential enemies, and may have developed from the need for rallying war-cries to urge men and camels into battle. Poets often boasted of their eagerness to kill—but never to die.

In a qasida each line ends with the same rhyme (some 30–120 lines), which compels the poet to use cross-rhymes and rhythms to hold his listeners' attention. In reciting or chanting, this monorhyme builds up impressively, particularly when used in dirge or elegy. The poem is a string of beads on which images are accumulated and juxtaposed one after the other without any seeming connection beyond that of a strict quantitative meter. The links are psychological and poetic; experiences held in common by poet and listener—tribal raids, sorrow at departing guests, love, desert floods, heroic deeds, generosity, cowardice, and succinct reflections on life's brevity. The power of the qasida lies in its directness, unimaginativeness even, the honor and praise of things seen and observed accurately, all expressed vividly but laconically—a series of swift images serving as mnemonic devices for the listener who can then say along with the poet: "Yes. That is so. I too have seen it. Therefore it is good poetry." Each recitation tested a poem's truth—listeners would note and disapprove inaccurate or imprecise images immediately, as they would departures from the form's strict meter. No poet could get away with inaccurate observation. Imagination (as Blake might have used the term) or eighteenth-century "fancy" had no place in the earliest Arabic poetry, nor did symbolism. The poet observed the similar in the dissimilar and vice versa—eyes weeping are not *like* waterskins with holes—they *are*; hence the vigor of these early poems.

An important variant of the qasida is the elegy or memorial poem for the dead. Used in this manner, the opening love-passage is cut out, as is the abusive section at the end, and the subject matter is adapted to suit the occasion. The incantatory momentum in these dirges is vital, for with nothing new to say about death, only simplicity and rhythmic musicality affects those in sorrow. The poetess, al-Khansa' (d. 644/5), wrote some of the best-known dirges in Arabic on the deaths of her two brothers in tribal skirmishes. Laments for the dead, except as literary exercises, are rare in English literature. The Mass, funeral oration, and memorial service serve in their stead.

The seeming lack of sustained subject makes it difficult to present an entire qasida so that the Western reader can feel the intensity and occasion of the poem, and the plausibility of the emotions expressed. My solution has been to limit the number of subjects touched on, or to divide the sections into separate poems. (Some scholars may object.)

In 622 A.D. Muhammad, the prophet of Islam, fled from Mecca to Medina, from which date the Muslim lunar calendar is calculated. Within one hundred years the Arabs had overthrown the Sasanid empire of Persia; expelled the Byzantines from Syria,

Egypt, and North Africa; and the Visigoths from southernmost Spain; taking with them their new faith, Islam, and their holy book, the Qur'an.

To the believing Muslim the Qur'an is the Word of God as revealed to the prophet Muhammad by the angel Gabriel, and Islam, "submission to the will of Allah," is the faith of one who submits, i.e. a Muslim, and all interpretations of this Will are founded on the Qur'an. Some chapters are solely prophetic and mystical, but others contain long sections on social legislation for this world—both aspects profoundly needed at that particular moment.

Although the Qur'an contains much fine poetry, even in translation, Muhammad protested strongly against being called a poet by his contemporaries because he wished to dissociate himself and the new faith from pagan tribal poets with their primitive polytheistic ways. Despite these protestations the Qur'an has had enormous influence on Arabic poetry, indeed on all Muslim literature. Allusions and quotations are common, with all the concomitant overtones and undercurrents—much as with the Bible in English literature. The cadence and imagery of the Qur'an have influenced Arabic poetry fundamentally.

The existence of the Qur'an has created vast categories of Arabic writing quite apart from poetry, devoted exclusively to Qur'anic studies: lexicography, biography, theology, philology, and law—all inspired by the Faithful to analyze and clarify the social and theological implications of the Qur'an, which, as the Word of God, was considered worthy of endless study and interpretation. Certainly Arabic would never have become the widespread language it is today without the Qur'an to focus and standardize it, for this single book is still the fountain of Islamic faith from Morocco to Indonesia. (The most reliable modern English translation is by Marmaduke Pickthall, *The Meaning of the Glorious Koran*, Mentor Books, MQ 375. It is best to read the final, i.e. shortest, chapters first.)

Social legislation in the Qur'an and all-pervading economic and political changes of the period radically altered the substance of Arabic poetry. At first a pious poetry developed, written in praise of Allah, the prophet, his mantle, and the achievements and blessings of Islam. This religious fervor shows itself particularly in the mixing of the sacred and profane in a single poem, as in Donne. In Western poetry the religious and secular tend to be kept apart, but to the orthodox Muslim no dichotomy appears to exist since every aspect of life is part of God's will and therefore sacred.

With the rise of the Umayyad dynasty to power in Damascus (661–750), tribal influences waned and Damascus, Basra, Kufa, and other cities superseded the Hijaz in Saudi Arabia, previously the traditional home of poets. This new urban life rendered much pre-Islamic poetry meaningless and irrelevant. Abandoned campsites, shifting sand-dunes, sand-grouse, and ostriches were sights unknown to most city-poets, who found the integrity of the emotions forced on the Bedouin, living intensely on a narrow front, extreme. They soon replaced these simpler desert reactions with the creation of artificial passionate loves, preferring the sweetness of love-lyrics to Bedouin austerity and directness of emotion. Poetry was no longer the beast of burden for each tribe's history; and wit, a certain levity, and poetic clowning came to the fore, but with idealized love still a constant theme.

In pre-Islamic poetry no man was ever praised but for what was in him, but with the rise of local courts, eulogies on influential men increased—to pay for a poet's food, lodgings, and warm winter cloak. Literary battles flourished, and the delight of poets in out-poetizing one another often led to scandalous verbal and sometimes physical attacks on poet-adversaries. The generous flow of obscenities in this jibing has made much Arabic poetry unpalatable to Western scholars and, with them as arbiters, to the West. (Likewise, the Rabelaisian realism in Sanskrit and Japanese *Edo* satirical verse tends to strike us as crude, unimaginative, and lacking in subtlety.)

The Umayyad Muslims invaded Spain (then under the Visigoths) from North Africa in 711 A.D. and remained—sometimes dominant, sometimes on the defensive, and later on fragmenting into separate minor dynasties—until all were finally ousted in 1492. In general the Christians held the northwest and the Muslims the south.

Religious leaders, sent by the Umayyads of Damascus to try to maintain the minimum standard of Arabic and religious knowledge expected of all Muslims, brought with them their theology and a taste for the contemporary poetry of their communities, particularly the love-poetry of the period. It was this poetry that the Arabs of Spain knew and imitated; in fact, it was not until the eleventh century that Andalusian poetry (that is, Arabic poetry written in Spain), acquired a coloring and flavor of its own, setting it apart from the poetry of the East. This Andalusian school emphasized the beauties of nature, gardens, and waterfalls, with a lyrical simplicity and delicate floral quality—a marked change from the formal, more ornate Eastern style. Although written at the sophisticated Muslim courts of Cordoba, Granada, Seville, and other centers, this new poetry, for singing and dancing to, brought in many popular elements, creating an exclusively Andalusian form, the *muwashshah*—Arabic but with colloquialisms from the popular Romance poetry of Spain. Such colloquialisms are very rare in Eastern Arabic poetry. Other regional forms developed, too.

One work of great interest is *The Dove's Neckring about Love and Lovers* by Ibn Hazm (993–1064), a distinguished Andalusian theologian. It is one of the most perspicacious analytical treatises on the psychology of love known. Although it is prose, Ibn Hazm included many poems, mostly his own, as commentary. It is essential reading if one is to understand the chivalric and courtly traditions of love in Arabic and Provençal poetry. The little poem I include from this work is quintessential Ibn Hazm: delicate, guileless, and astute.

Only in recent years have scholars begun to unravel the mutual influences of Arabic and Spanish poetry. Bilingualism was normal in Spain for at least two or three centuries, and although Spanish and Arabic poetry lived back to back over most of this period, the reciprocal influences seem to have varied from court to court and poet to poet. Some Arabic poetry was interlarded with Spanish words; some Spanish verse was in Arabic script and full of Arabic; a little Arabic poetry is even known to have been written in the "Christian style" (i.e. in Roman letters); and a modern scholar (S. M. Stern) writes learnedly of Hebrew imitations of Arabic poems, which may have ultimately influenced Spanish poetry itself. This is not surprising since some of the Muslim courts were significant centers for translating Arabic into Latin, the work being done by learned members of the extensive Jewish communities in Spain.

It has even been suggested that Hebrew-Spanish poetry may be one of the possible links between Arabic and Provençal poetry, but the whole problem of the Arabic influence on Provençal and Troubadour poetry still needs much original work on manuscripts. For instance, the Arabic root, *TaRiBa*, "to be overjoyed," and in other forms meaning "to sing or chant," may possibly be related to *TRouBadour*, through the Provençal *TRoBar*, but this is still disputed and inadequately documented; all of which raises the further complex question of Islamic influences on mediaeval Christian thought and philosophy, particularly on Dante (1265–1321). For example, Dante's scheme of the Hereafter in the *Divine Comedy* closely parallels a work by the important Andalusian mystic and poet, Ibn al-Arabi (1165–1240), who wrote an account of Muhammad's ascent to Heaven, and other contemporary popular accounts in Latin and French based on Arabic sources. (See works by Cerulli, Levi Della Vida; and M. Rodinson, article in Pearson, No. 23275.) Eventually our knowledge of mediaeval Europe will have to be re-assessed in the light of accumulating evidence that the Muslims in Spain contributed greatly to the enlightenment of Europe.

With the fall of the Umayyads of Damascus in 750 A.D., the Abbasids came to power, with Baghdad their focus—until the Mongols destroyed both city and dynasty in 1258. Under the Abbasids, who emanated predominantly from Eastern Persia and Khurasan, the Persian influence increased greatly. They had a growing empire to cope with—taxes to collect, a postal system to maintain, and Islamic law to enforce—for which they used the Sasanid administrative system still extant in Persia, but they had to rely on Persians to run it. The marriage of Arab and Persian, in literature and the homes, created one of the most luxuriant and exhilarating periods in history, symbolized in the name of Harun al-Rashid, the caliph of Baghdad (d. 809 A.D.).

Islam had spread so rapidly, and in some places so superficially, that the Arabs soon became alarmed at the deterioration in the standard of Arabic. Abbasid scholars and historians were urged to collect, collate, and edit the works of earlier poets as samples of "pure" Arabic, from which they deduced grammatical rules of great intricacy that have remained ever since. It was under the Abbasids that the major lexicographers started their dictionaries, listing words, not alphabetically, but according to their root letters—a system still used today. These lexicographers and grammarians were chiefly concerned with educating non-Arabs to speak and write Arabic correctly, and were humanist in their intent. To the Arab, a grammarian was not a dry-as-dust scholar, but biographer, literary critic, cultivated lecturer, and poet in his own right.

Idolization of pre-Islamic Bedouin poets by men of this period who knew nothing of desert life produced much bad poetry—sterile imitations of their own classics; but alongside this there developed an exotic imagery, ornate and intricate, full of "conceits" and sophisticated technique, in men such as Mutanabbi (915–965). Arabs still admire Mutanabbi greatly, but he is difficult for Westerners to assimilate. This imagery increasingly dominated love-poetry, which developed rapidly, probably influenced by the Persian taste for chivalry and courtly love—tedious when poorly handled but remarkably fine when perceptive. Some of the best poetry of this period was satire and social criticism: satires of classical Bedouin qasidas, as in Abu Nuwas (d. 815?), and epigrammatic commentaries on society, as in Ibn al-Rumi (836–896)—both men close to Martial and Juvenal in spirit.

By later Abbasid times poets, fed up with arbitrary treatment at court and stifled by a luxury they may have wished their own, withdrew into a semi-religious Sufi mysticism. Prompted by much political uncertainty, this mysticism began to encroach on all Arabic poetry, particularly in Muslim Spain. It even permeated the prose and by about 1200 had undermined the poetry, but this mystical spirit found further outlets in Persia where it was the source of some remarkable works—until ultimately it stultified Persian poetry too.

Arabic poetry and literature in general declined rapidly after the Mongols destroyed Baghdad in 1258. Only a few important Arab writers come later, notably the historian Ibn Khaldun (1332–1406). Classical Arabic poetry came to an end, but the poetic tradition in Islam continued and developed independently in Persia, Turkey, and the Mughal empire. It was not until the latter half of the nineteenth century that Arabic poetry revived, with marked European influences. This revival continues today.

Persian Poetry

850 – 1400 A.D.

Persian is an Indo-European language, and therefore differs considerably in structure from Arabic, a Semitic one. It is much more idiomatic and colloquial. Persian is easy to rhyme because the sentence usually ends with a verb, which limits the variety possible. It is a superb language for puns, *double entendre*, and all the tricks of a crossword-puzzler; but the poetry itself is sweeter, subtler, and more reflective than the more masculine Arabic poetry. This musical quality makes it almost impossible to re-create Persian poems in another tongue; their spirit is far more elusive and complex than that of Arabic ones, for the mellifluous quality of the language tends to turn the poems into "pure" sound, sometimes with rather slight meaning attached. Despite this emphasis on sound, Persians often achieve the rare accomplishment of melting poetry and philosophy in one crucible.

Persian philosophy is far more skeptical, dualistic, and heretical than that of the Arabs, and religious heresy appears to be endemic among Persians for whom this universe is a sorry trick played on man: "this is a world of sorrow...and the sooner we leave it for elsewhere the better...but be patient...life is but a beggar's gift." To complement this skepticism much of the poetry, except for the earliest, contains a profound and sometimes very moving mystical faith. This mystical element tends to dominate in times of political upheaval and exceptional tyranny, and since Persian political history is essentially that of one arbitrary tyrant after another, Persian poetry has retained mysticism, tempered with skepticism, as a vital force for a long time. Tyranny seems to compel men to seek something outside themselves and in so doing to renounce this world, turn mystic, and await their full recompense in the next. Persians have long known that one can be surrounded by tyrants and still think thoughts freely—so long as they are clothed in the decent obscurity of mystical poetic language.

Beginning about 637 A.D. the Arabs conquered Persia, overthrowing the Sasanid dynasty which had worn itself out warring against the Byzantine empire to the northwest. As is to be expected when invaders overrun an older civilization, the Arab newcomers inevitably adopted much of the culture they found. The desert Arab invaders, or lizard-eaters as the Persians called them, had nothing to offer an ancient civilization except Islam and the Arabic script. The Persians quickly adopted the new script to replace their own highly complicated and inefficient Pehlevi (one of the most ambiguous scripts ever to exist); and Islam, sometimes in a schismatic form (Shi'ism), soon became the dominant faith in Persia. The Arab military conquest of Persia became the Persian cultural conquest of the Arabs, particularly after 750 A.D. under the Abbasids when Persian influence permeated the court at Baghdad, the literature, and the complex administration of an empire.

The introduction of Arabic script made possible a great upsurge of poetry written by Persians. With literacy no longer confined to Zoroastrian priests for copying the Avesta and other religious writings, Persian poetry written in Arabic script began to flow by about 850—probably earlier, but little remains. Rudaki (870?–940/1), the most interesting of the early poets, wrote simply with a minimum Arabic vocabulary. His language is probably closer to rural Persian of today than Elizabethan English is to a Londoner or Bostonian; likewise Firdawsi (d. 1020), who wrote the enormous epic, the *Shahnameh* ("Book of Kings"), used a limited Arabic vocabulary.

The Arabic influence on Persian poetry was vast and complex, and the reciprocal influence equally important. Language was never a barrier between these two literatures for, as is often true in the Orient, religious boundaries are more significant in literature than are linguistic ones. Often a Persian writer's first language was Arabic. Ibn Sina (980–1037), the great Persian philosopher known to Dante and the West as Avicenna, wrote his poem on the Soul, and most of his other works, in Arabic. Most Persian poets wrote in both languages, and translated their own works easily from one to the other. They introduced the quatrain (*ruba'i*, pl. *ruba'iyat*), exclusively a Persian form, into Arabic by translating their own verses. This particular form was used most effectively by Abu'l Ala al-Ma'arri, the Syrian poet (973–1057), for his skeptical verses in Arabic. The Persians adopted Arabic poetic forms readily, especially the qasida, but the cadence of their language demanded innovations. Minuchihri (d. 1041) used the qasida form extensively, but his poems have all the movement of Persian, not of Arabic. In general, the qasida became recognized as an accepted "Persian" form. Conversely, the *ghazal*, a short love-lyric, widely used by the Arabs, is believed to have been Persian in origin. The Arabs never borrowed the epic, and no one seems to know why.

With political disenchantment under the later Abbasids, Persians returned more and more to their own tongue, becoming circuitous and deliberate in obscuring their meaning—if only to save their heads. Embellishment and pomposity of style became the norm at court. The simpler poetry of the earliest period was ignored—Rudaki forgotten. Taste had changed and vast quantities of the earliest poetry was lost. Despite the growing complexity, poetry still thrived in Persia whereas the same obscurity ultimately throttled Arabic poetry.

Persian poetry is more varied than Arabic in subject matter, for the Persians had a long pre-Islamic royalist tradition from which they disentangled epics, filled with long dualistic mythological tales. The best of these epics, Firdawsi's *Shahnameh* ("Book of Kings") is written in simple language and is full of good yarns. (Reuben Levy's translation in prose (1967) occasionally catches the spirit better than any of the poetic versions so far, and is worth dipping into.) The Persians also had their gardens and their *naw-ruz* ("new day"). This is the first day of the Persian solar New Year (March 21st) and the first day of Spring: a time for picnics, festivities, and family reunions—and for centuries a traditional subject for Persian poets. It is also an occasion for exchanging gifts, and no doubt poets at court hoped to exchange their poems welcoming in the Spring and New Year for more substantial things. This renewal of earth's bounty, the blossoming of the first flowers in a garden—in a country largely desert—is a wonderful sight and great joy; and all Persians, not only their poets, celebrate their love of intricate beauty on such occasions.

This love of intricacy is in all the Persian arts: a garden-like filigree of finely-wrought detail, in their carpets, their mosques, ceramic tiles, metal-work, illuminated manuscripts, and miniatures. These are all created out of a subtlety and delicacy peculiarly Persian. Hidden within this delicacy their poems contain much symbolism: the nightingale, the ephemeral rose with its fragrance and ever-present thorns, wine, the wine-cup, and its bearer. These symbols have become so traditional that whenever used they refer to a cluster of meanings, immediate to a Persian reader but lost on the Westerner.

Most Persian lyrical and mystical poems are static statements of imagist detail about the lover and the beloved. The lover and beloved are types, not individuals. Accept this, and much seeming dullness in Persian and other oriental poetry vanishes. The lover, always distraught and in anguish at imagined slights and inattentions, a slave to love's call, suffers joyfully and eagerly for the haughty beloved who accepts every attention as her due, and is entirely at liberty to glance or not on her lover at whim, without concern for his feelings. The Persian poet describes in joy his longings and his sorrows. This total subservience of the lover is then likened to man's complete dependence on God, and from there any combination of symbols is possible. Another favorite group of images comes from the Persian game of polo: God is the polo-stick, man the ball, battered and beaten by God into submission—or the Potter and His clay.

The symbolism that develops in later Persian mystical poetry is complex: making the abstract physical and spiritualizing the visible; and often it is impossible to say whether the "love" referred to is the soul, the love of God, a beautiful girl, a handsome youth, or simply the wine itself and the pleasure of drinking it. Some scholars believe the poets themselves were uncertain. In the West, Donne's harmonizing of the erotic and theological is perhaps the nearest one can get to the mood of Persian mystical poetry—"the sacred impiety of Persian poetry," as a distinguished

Italian scholar calls it. Symbolism sterilized much Persian poetry, for with the accumulation of overtones, the symbol came to mean more than what it had represented originally, and poets wrote about the symbol rather than what it stood for.

The deliberate avoidance of originality bores us in the West, but then originality in poetry is a Western concept, alien to the Persian—in whose poetry people are never individuals but universals, stylized beings (the lover, the beloved, etc.), characteristic of all humans. To improve on the poems of his forerunners, to repeat them in refined forms, arouses in the Persian an intensity of literary associations and allusions unknown to non-Persians, but possibly akin to the Japanese reading their own *haiku*.

In this small selection of Persian poems many great names are missing: Firdawsi (d. 1020), Sa'di (1193?–1291?), Hafiz (1325?–1390?), Jami (1414–1492), and Omar Khayyam (1048–1131). Firdawsi's epic needs long passages to be effective; Sa'di's poetry (as distinct from his prose) is a serious omission and noted as such; Hafiz seems to me untranslatable—the music vanishes and the gossamer left behind soon evaporates; Jami is too lush for me; and, but for Fitzgerald, Khayyam's only significance would be as a distinguished astronomer and mathematician. Omar's contemporaries considered him next to Ibn Sina (Avicenna) in learning, especially in astronomy, algebra, and theology, but they disliked him for being ill-tempered, peevish, and garrulous. They also note that he wrote poetry (in Persian and Arabic), but his quatrains (*ruba'iyat*)—taut perceptions, some hedonist, others Sufi and mystical, written from early youth to old age—were mostly ignored as being unworthy of such a learned man.

Khayyam first became known in Europe in 1700—as an astronomer and reformer of the Persian calendar—through translation into Latin of biographical notes and one quatrain (spurious?) in a Persian manuscript at Oxford. 150 years later (1851), a French scholar translated a treatise by Khayyam on algebra, and in 1859 Fitzgerald published his first version of *The Rubaiyat*, privately and anonymously. It was ignored and remaindered. Then in 1867 J. B. Nicolas, French Consul at Resht, published a scholarly edition of 464 quatrains with French translation, in time for Fitzgerald to emend his second edition (1868) which caught the imagination of Europe.

Fitzgerald's success was Omar's, and since then scholars have been searching manuscripts trying to reconstruct an authentic text. No single early manuscript exists, only excerpts from other works and anthologies. The earliest known quatrains (only two) that seem to be authentic come from a Leningrad manuscript dated about 1200, and the oldest manuscript devoted exclusively to a collection of his quatrains is dated 1340–1, which is as though the oldest manuscript of *The Canterbury Tales* dated from Shakespeare's times. The later the manuscript the more the quatrains attributed to Omar accumulate, and scholars differ on how many may be by him—from only three up to 1700. Arberry's estimate of at least 250 seems the best judgment to date. (For details, see Christensen, Csillik, Minorsky, and Arberry. Also article by J. A. Boyle, "Omar Khayyam....", in *Bulletin of the John Rylands Library, Vol.* 52, *No.* 1, *Autumn*, 1969.) Forgeries of manuscripts are also known: four "important" ones, reputedly dated between 1208 and 1259, were probably forged in Tehran (1947–52) for the New York antiquarian market (see Minorsky in *Yadname-ye Jan Rypka*, Prague, 1967—in English). Such forgeries are useful, since scholars enjoy unmasking them and in so doing review the accumulated knowledge with greater precision and insight.

Arabic Poems

ABID IBN AL-ABRAS

Lament for an Arab Encampment

No head-ropes or dung
the Chandlers, Bakers
and Whitbys all gone
with death their only heirs.

Slaughtered and scattered
shame on greybeards left behind
my eyes seep sorrow,
waterskins with holes,
as I recall my first horse
and foal and that slip-of-a-thing
next door.

How can I stay and overlook a land
where water hurried
and sand-grouse scurried,
top-soil and all my people gone.

None to inherit herds
spoils despoiled
where even quick ones fail
and weaklings sometimes win.
Men cannot save those
who cannot learn from Time.

Help the land on which you live
where only judgment aids a man

don't groan and sigh,
        I am a stranger to this life,
for strangers sometimes bring
more than a kinsman turned strange can.

The longer we live
the more we deceive
ourselves and mourn,
long life   long trouble
what's left   is rubble.
        Pray to the gods
        but never beg of man.

An Arab Chieftain to His Young Wife

Enough complaining
more can wait till dawn
I may be worn in age
        need you tell me so?
but dammit, don't yawn.

Are you toying with divorce
or me? You were never coy
in all our nights before
when, as sand flows over dunes
we soon were one
        soft dunes
we soon were one.

But now you want a lad
to plow from evening prayer
through winter's night
to dawn,

you even doubt I was a man.
        Me!
I have worn out more bridles
stained more dawns with blood
and kissed more linen necks
than any plowboy you think tough

Come, leave off your frowns
peace can be ours my love,
          if that be enough.

AL-KHANSA'

Lament for a Brother

What have we done to you, death
that you treat us so,
with always another catch
one day a warrior
the next a head of state;
charmed by the loyal
you choose the best.
Iniquitous, unequalling death
I would not complain
if you were just
but you take the worthy
leaving fools for us.

Fifty years among us
upholding rights
annulling wrongs,
impatient death
could you not wait
                    a little longer.
He still would be here
and mine, a brother
without a flaw. Peace
be upon him and Spring
rains water his tomb
                    but
could you not wait
                    a little longer
                    a little longer,
you came too soon.

AL-HUTAY'A

It Is New

It is new
therefore a pleasure,

and death?
is that also
cordial
and sugar?

ABU DHU'AYB AL-HUDHALI

Lament for Five Sons Lost in a Plague

Run down by fate's spite
my body hangs, a mantle on a broom;

with wealth enough to ease all pain
I turn at night from back to belly
side after side after side.
Who put pebbles on my couch when my sons died?

I tried but could not shield
them well enough from fate
whose talon-grip
turns amulet to toy.

Thorns tear out my eyes. I lie,
a flagstone at the feet of Time
all men wear me down
but even those my pain delights
envy that I cannot cringe
at fortune's spite.

JAMÍL

Salsabíl

a fountain in Paradise whose waters
contain no roughness and slip readily
down the throat. Also, a girl's name.

I keep saying:
shame on all other men
with their loves
succeeding one another;

and still
you will not let me
marry your daughter.

Then I must drink deep
yessir! drink deep of her
                    to my successor.

And after
                    dream of twigs
and wisps of straw upstream
that soon will clog clear water.

AL-TIRIMMAH

In the Heart of the Desert

A foolish man rides here
with my saddle
and on my camel.

Lord of the Throne

Lord of the throne
if death be near
don't take me off
on a couch of silk,
let me die ambushed
in a water-course
with men
all serving
Allah's ends around,
my head slashed off
my flesh worthy
of cleansing vulture
and hovering kite,
my bones soon blasted
dry and white.

DHU'L-RUMMA

Of All Garments

Of all garments
God blast the veil

it hides beauty
to incite the young

and masks the vile
to urge us on.
God blast the veil.

KUTHAIYIR

At Her Grave

My donkey stops
tears loiter too
as I manage to say
Allah be merciful to you . . .

When she was away
living was hell
and I always cried.

Today. Look at me. All rags.
It's just as well she died.

MUZAHIM AL-UQAILI

The Earth Outside

The earth outside
spun within
when they told me
she had married him.

Now I know it's over
but Allah,
Why did you let her go?
To pity what is left of me
and emphasize you still control?

Be merciful to her
through him.

He must have been poor indeed
to need her more than I.

ABU DULAMA

Behold My Mother!

Behold my mother!
A camel at her master's tomb
a demon's shadow
starved to a witch's broom;

her only fortune: me,
five laying hens
one white goat
a scabby camel
and two gelded cocks.

Her letters with her scorpion seal
reek of misfortune and socks.

Al-Mansur!
Caliph and builder of Baghdad
Allah be merciful to her through you
bring moisture
from your clouds of generosity
O giver and son
of a hero's son,
son of a hero's tribe,
son of those who aided Allah
in grave events now past,
do not let His stallions
lunge and dart at her
through mist and dust.

Traders in Beauty and Delight

You want a soothing life
all beauty and no worry,
what's sweeter then
than writing poetry?

Misfortune rakes poets
they gulp ill-luck
cup after cup
till broke
then turn to slavery
to stave off bankruptcy
and buy a winter cloak.

Try buying slaves instead
trading in rounded breasts
or manly gestures,
a profit's sure
no need to borrow
nothing to store or kill
a wedding every night,
the merchandise for sale
tomorrow.

ABU NUWAS

The Rake

an imitation of abu nuwas

Abandoned camps
pineapple breasts untouched
camels too young to die in battle
boys grown hairy
stallions lost
lovers parting with caravans at dawn;
Nuts! That's all stuff for poetry,
                unlike my sorrow.

For be there any sorrow more than mine?
The Prophet, may his name be ever blessed,
bans wine, and worse
                the magistrates enforce it.

Mix it with tears
yours
mine
I don't care whose
I'll drink and wait
nightwatchmen to pick me up
and bastinado me;
        guardians of my purity.

Fools, why not let me be,
drinking with every toy in town,
                don't thwart Allah

the world could end tomorrow
with you regretting purity,
while I will surely be
worthy of His Clemency.

AL-ABBAS IBN AL-AHNAF

Love

Dear love
'tis less than I have vowed
but let me gather in
and bring
all love
from earth and sea and sky;

then
let us to its equalling
that love,
when death has ravished us,
encase our shroud.

IBN AL-RUMI

Slow Giving

re that winter cloak
I often beg you for,
please!
I never said "shroud,"
and need it now
upon-my-soul
before my body leaves.

The Weighing-In

Fortune always boosts the dumb
and downs those with merit
the balance sinks with gravity
and up come those
who dote on levity and vanity,
the living drown
and leave the dead afloat.

The Compromise

He dyes
his white hair black
in part,
believing some
will think him wise
and others
young.

To a Hunchback

Attributed

It is no fault to be deformed
drawn ligaments create the crescent moon
the viol's curvature rewards
nights and feasts with song and sleep
the bow's more feared than Christian sword
and scimitar more sure,
the camel with a swollen hump studs most
and only prows can split the waves.

The gods endow you hunchbacks
with virtues
as hillocks on a mountain-top
and women, when they see
such superfluities,
devote themselves to men
who
arch
like
you.

MUTANABBI

Shame Kept My Tears Away

Shame kept my tears away
but's brought them back again.
My veins and bones seep through the skin
graining *her* iv'ry face
with lines anew.

Unveiling shows pale veil beneath
as woman's Rhetorick
of inlaid gold and pearl
in filigree marks cheek
and jowl.

Her night of hair she parts in three
(to make for me four nights of one?);
pale moon reflects her day of face,
that she and I may double see
as one.

AL-LAJJAM AL-HARRANI

His Banquets Cure Most Ills

His banquets cure most ills
with their herbs and other simples,
bread sliced thin
meat diced fine
each morsel counted
lest the servants dine.

If asked to dinner—
            eat first,
or grow thinner.

AL-IFRIQI AL-MUTAYYAM

My Wife Complains I Pray No More

My wife complains I pray no more.
What! me pray to God!
I'm too poor,
nothing to protect
no bins of wine, Nash house
or chests of silver
by Paul Storr.

Pray well, Mr. Getty
pray well, Mr. Clore
protect your city sites
and ore
and tell the gods that I,
no hypocrite,
(call me a drunkard and a fool,)
will pray again
when I possess what other men
can take away again
and store.

Oh God! drag me from my misery,
sincere but poor.

UNKNOWN

Waves

Waves
bow
before
the shore

courtiers
to their king

and then
withdraw.

IBN HAZM AL-ANDALUSI

Twice Times Then is Now

You ask how old am I
bleached by the sun
my teeth all gone.
How old am I?

I have no guide
no calendar inside
except a smile
and little kiss
she gave me
by surprise
upon my brow.

And now,
that little while
is all my life
and all reality,
how long or brief
it seems to be.

ABU ISHAQ AL-ILBIRI

Granada (1000 A.D.)

For Agnes Bedford

One after the other
my contemporaries die,
I know I shall not live for ever
but even as I touch
the coffin's cotton quilt
I feel so far from them
I cannot even choose
to be a looker-on,
but only see as one
who suddenly awakes
and walks with eyes
still shut, towards the light.

Another funeral done
now back to my hut
with wolves nearby
far safer than friends at court
where my contemporaries
all seem to die.

I remember leaving them
times were so unjust
those first were never men of worth
and those last, for ever
pushing on and up, were worse.

So I stayed aloof
finding none I'd care
to share my supper with
                    or an evening prayer.

And now some younger ones
from the city come bustling in
saying it isn't right
that I, a learned man,
should end thus; perhaps
they also think they wear
a corner of my cloak
when they see their friends
in court at ease.

So they fuss
about a house for me,
well-meaning I suppose
and it's nice to have some,
especially the young,
respectful at last, even though
they sometimes interrupt a doze.

But they don't understand,
my hut's more than enough
for one soon to die.

Tomorrow I'll tell them again:
but for summer heat, and rain,
occasional thieves in my garden,
and odds and ends the women need,
I'd build myself a spider's house;
I won't mention that my hands
are too arthritic to weave.

Persian Poems

RUDAKI

Young or Old We Die

Young or old we die
for every neck a noose
though the rope be long for some,

struggle or calm
broke or a king
life's but wind
        and a dream
perhaps describing
some other thing;

and with the end
all will be the same again
and all will be well.

Quatrain

With you away—despair!
but even then my joy
in caring
is more than all my sorrow.

If away my joy is such, what then
when you return
        tomorrow.

MINUCHIHRI

Recantation

I'm through with acid and with praise
my satire's wasted and panegyric never pays
I call them niggards (they think this eulogy)
but when I note their lusts and avarice
they smile upon this ageing satirist.

Before my time
poets and singers soon aroused
love, worthy of vellum and private presses,
and even customs men wrote verses
with music in each noble line:

Whan that Aprille with his shoures soote . . .
Rough winds do shake the darling buds of May . . .
And did those feet . . .
Into the valley of . . .
Death, be not proud . . .
Pull down thy vanity, I say, pull down . . .

But now?
It's all Betjeman, Ginsberg and Ogden Nash
guitars and Trinidaddy drums
metal drums, rhythm without song
hum-drumming poets out of town
and leaving none to honor men,
                events
                and verse,

while those who stay behind
call poetry "all lies for cash."
Will they never learn,
if all praise be lies,
the Prophet was never born
and cities never sacked.

Demon in Paradise

Tell me, why such a foul mood?
If I speak gently you take offence or cry,
my kindnesses you count all lies.

Sorry, I murmur, as I try . . .
Why, you grunt, apologize?
Cut out all the platitudes,
astringent as honey
from the eucalyptus tree,
for me
　　　　our hour together lasts just that,
for you
　　　　its overspill will bring you back.

I Send You My Verses

I send you my verses
citing passion without passion,
three this week and two before.

Perhaps you do not like the stuff
or blush. Your silence
gives me no excuse for more.

RASHIDI SAMARQANDI

Complaint to a Court Poet

You say my poetry
lacks spice
not enough Freud
and too little vice.
You may be right.

My lines are soft and sweet as new-mown hay
just the place for nature's play.

I leave to you
the public's taste
for sorrel, vinegar
and human waste.

Hors de Combat

For T. S. B.

the poet politely refuses
recall to the royal palace.

Even gods resent my paradise
a cottage with thrushes in the loft
and senior civil servants beg me back
to dine at Claridges
and view the dogs at Cruft's.

But with Wensleydale and Granny Smiths
black walnuts and valley mists
the government must do without;

non-patriot and wrong though I may be
in the locust's foot is my well-being
and more's too much for me.

What I wear (burlap for cotton)
and where I live
answer best your plea,
there's envy enough at court
without one arrayed like me.

NIZAMI ARUDI

Calling the Doctor (1000 A.D.)

For Basil Bunting

1

Go find Avicenna
　　or my son will die,
make forty copies of this miniature,
don't paint alembics in his lap
or gardens with mauve rocks behind.
　　Damn court artists
　　their frills and fuss.
Just his features, enough,
that will give you fewer lines
to fight about.
Send one to every court
　　but get them off tonight
with the royal command:
Abu ali ibn sina is sought
　　and must be found.

2

You've found him.
　　What!
chuckling to himself. How dare he
with my son about to . . .
　　　　and what?

asking if birds fly through sandstorms
or around,
chuckling indeed
I'll chuckle him,
go bring him in.
Stop it, rings
don't sparkle so. Yours is not the light
to hustle him.

3

Ruler of the world! Your majesty desires?
. . . my son, with the first fuzz of youth
around his chin is
you understand
about to
die,
my son,
the king's son,
come and examine him.

Rings, stop jangling like jays.
I wonder which is worse
private or public pain,
a king's a child where children reign.

4

The lad seems worn,
pulse regular, urine opaque.
That was a fine amber ring
the king wore. No wonder he attracts
such chaff. I'm one straw more.
The boy's so thin, withdrawn,
with saffron down around his chin.

. . . that's odd, before I mention
the disease I know the cure.
I knew more at ten

than he will ever know, but Muhammad,
Seal of all Prophets,
tell me more about the soul;
is it within or out, and must I doubt
before I know, or will doubt kill
all knowing?
The soul needs reason,
and reason, knowing.

Your majesty, send me a man
who knows the town.

5

You're the city clerk?
Now list
slowly, please
the quarters of the town;
boy
your wrist
don't worry
it's not to bleed you
just to take your pulse again.

Clerk
you were saying?
the gate to Mazanderan
the Prophet's gate, and Newgate
the oldest one in town,

fine, now list the roads that lead
to Mazanderan: Cobbler's Way,
Bread alley and Indigo lane.

Right! now recite from tax lists
if you can
each household in Indigo lane:

the Jasmine estate, Thanks-be-to-God,
Hassan Firuz, Godspeed, Makepeace
and Worthy the scribe

Stop!

That's enough, clerk, take this
for your trouble. Goodbye son,
I'm done and off to tell your father
the cure to kill what's ailing you.

6

Your majesty, I cannot hide
behind incantations, spells
and magic lore,
not that I dismiss prayer
to set a man right,
your son will soon be well
with eyes bright
as alhazen's reflected light:
his sickness: pride.
He has a secret love
and none he thought loved like him before,
and telling none
he's burning down;
it's Worthy the scribe's daughter
in Indigo lane by the gate to Mazanderan.
The cure? Arrange a feast, proclaim he's cured,
announce the wedding soon
he'll be up by noon,
and don't ask how
I named the bride.

You need no medico for that. I knew
he'd surely lie if asked the name
for which he'd gladly die,
but as your clerk,
promote him if you wish,

reeled off gates and streets
the pulse would change, and soon
I knew her name. May she be worthy
of your own.

7

My reward?
Three scribes dumb enough
to copy down exactly what I say
and not what they think I've said,
and a girl from Samarqand
for my bed.

JAMAL ISFAHANI

White Hairs

White hairs
are the voice
of the wind of death
and with them comes
despair

they shudder the willow
of my heart—and moan:

What! Still asleep!
You're no longer needed here,
it is time to leave for home.

JALAL AL-DIN RUMI

Quatrain

I cry:
but you want comforting

I am silent:
you hope for tears

I joust:
"keep still" you say

and in my lassitude
you'd have me up and do.

Why this autumn chill
where I expected Spring?

KEMAL KHOJANDI

One Final Fling

a restatement of a point of view

Wind in your hair
my palms and fingers plow
through and through and through,
oh, god live for ever
young and beautiful.

my fingers plow . . .

You turn my winter into spring
and all I bring: tears for lips
that hold my tongue. Stay young
even if not for me, stay young.

Soon you must go
and leave me living
like the blind
feeling but the edge of things
until my final burst
of dying brings
the luxury of death,
before I grow unkind.

Biographical Notes

Encyclopaedia of Islam, 4 vols. and suppl. 1913–38.
Encyclopaedia of Islam, New Edition, 2 vols. to date, 1954–.
Shorter Encyclopaedia of Islam, Leiden, 1953.
R. Blachère, *Histoire de la Littérature Arabe des Origines à la fin du XVe siècle de J.-C.*, 3 vols. to date, 1954, 1964, 1966–.
E. G. Browne, *A Literary History of Persia*, 4 vols., 1902–24.
I. M. Filshtinsky, *Arabic Literature*, Moscow, 1966 (paperback).
H. A. R. Gibb, *Arabic Literature*, 2nd rev. ed., Oxford, 1963.
R. A. Nicholson, *A Literary History of the Arabs*, 1907.
J. Rypka, *A History of Iranian Literature*, Dordrecht (Holland), 1968.

For further biography and bibliography, see references after each note.

AL-ABBAS IBN AL-AHNAF
died 808?

Grew up in Baghdad. Accompanied Harun al-Rashid on military campaigns in Armenia and Khurasan (eastern Persia). Wrote mostly simple love lyrics, *ghazal*, and no panegyrics. He differs from his contemporary Abu Nuwas in that his lyrics are closer to Herrick and the Minnesingers. His influence on later Arabic poetry, particularly in Spain, was profound. Arabs still read him. "Al-Abbas ibn al-Ahnaf," *Encyclopaedia of Islam*, 1954–, Vol. I, pp. 9–10.

ABID IBN AL-ABRAS
about 500–550?

Probably died before fifty. His poems are generally austere, dignified, with much specific desert detail (head-ropes, sand-grouse, etc.) and reflections on the rapid passing of a man's life. His matter-of-fact detail creates durable simplicity. His love of the past is unsentimental but moving. Man's efforts appear insignifi-

cant pitted against winds and depredations of Time. Classical authors much admired his descriptions of desert storms. His love poems are also dignified, and the unspoiled intensity of his emotion excludes self-pity; his humanity is too profound for that. "Lament for an Arab Encampment" typifies his poems and many others of the period: man cannot win against nature, must live with it; and the brutal reality of tribal communities dispersed through erosion (hence lack of water). "An Arab Chieftain to his young Wife" is made up of two small sections on this subject, taken from longer poems. Theme, a perennial one: an old man unable to satisfy a young girl fully, and her insensitivity to his pride. He wants tranquillity in love; she, more.
"Abid ibn al-Abras," *Encyclopaedia of Islam*, 1954–, Vol. I, p. 99; Blachère, Vol. II, pp. 293–294; C. Lyall, *Diwan of Abid ibn al-Abras*, London, 1913.

ABU DHU'AYB AL-HUDHALI
died 649?

Reputation for concision and well-constructed poems justified. His "Lament for Five Sons Lost in a Plague" is still considered one of the great poems in Arabic. "Who put pebbles on my couch when my sons died?" How better to portray the fatigue of sorrow and its sleepless nights? No effusion, but an objective description of anguish and man's inability to cope with Fate. Despite his sorrow, note the Arab dignity and ability to bear tribulation.
"Abu Dhu'ayb al-Hudhali," *Encyclopaedia of Islam*, 1954–, Vol. I, p. 115; Blachère, Vol. II, pp. 281–282.

ABU DULAMA
died 776/7?

Probably born about 720–730, a black slave from Abyssinia, he spanned the change-over from Umayyads to Abbasids. Satirist, court jester, with acrid tongue and comic streak. Somewhat akin to Thomas Hood and Ogden Nash, but coarser and more Rabelaisian. Frequently blends sacred and profane in one poem. Seems to have spent most of his time writing dishonest praise to help

pay rent. His poems are vivid, nearly always amusing, and probably totally dishonest; but occasionally one sees through them the tragic clown, as in his plea for funds for his starving mother, said to have been spoken before al-Mansur who was handing out largesse to his followers after the building of Baghdad. His poems begin with praise and end with pleas (for money). He wrote a poem about his mule, well known to Arabs.
"Abu Dulama," *Encyclopaedia of Islam*, 1954–, Vol. I, p. 116; M. Ben Cheneb, *Abu Dolama*, Alger, 1922.

ABU ISHAQ AL-ILBIRI
died 1067

Born about 995. Learned Andalusian theologian, poet and political agitator. Died in exile in al-Ilbiri (Elvira), after refusing a court invitation to return to Granada to live in comfort. In "Granada" I have cut out a long tedious political diatribe, preferring to unite the personal elements scattered throughout the poem.
"Abu Ishaq al-Ilbiri," *Encyclopaedia of Islam*, 1954–, Vol. I, p. 130; see also works by Dozy, Henri Pérès and A. R. Nykl.

ABU NUWAS
747?–815?

Born in Ahwaz (on Persian Gulf), of a Persian mother. Went to Baghdad as young man but for political reasons fled to Egypt. Lived an exotic life, falling in love with young boys and girls. Wrote some fine poems, full of humour and understanding, mostly poems on love and wine. Readily admits his own defects and seems to be sustained by genuine religious belief that Allah will judge him fairly, for without his wrong-doings Allah's Clemency is wasted. Had no time for moralists who presumed to know what he should or should not do. His poems have greatly influenced modern Arab authors. He is somewhat akin to Rochester and the "Rake" poets of the seventeenth century. "The Rake" is an "imitation" put together from three different poems to illustrate his basic points of view. Wrote parodies of the classical

Arab poetry he disdained. Read "The Rake" alongside "Lament for an Arab Encampment."
"Abu Nuwas," *Encyclopaedia of Islam*, 1954–, Vol. I, pp. 143–144; Filshtinsky, pp. 91–96; Nicholson, pp. 292–296; Gibb, pp. 62–63.

ANVARI
1126–1189/90?

Born in Khurasan and probably buried at Balkh in central Asia. Courtiers thought less of his talents than he did. An excellent poet but obscure at times. Disillusioned with court intrigue he retired to countryside in his old age; was invited to return to court but, preferring the simple pleasures of his cottage, politely declined—which shows character, since to refuse a royal summons was tantamount to wishing one's head and body separated. "Locust's foot": an ant is said to have presented Solomon the most treasured possession of his poverty: a locust's leg. (Cf. the widow's mite.)
"Anwari," *Encyclopaedia of Islam*, 1954–, Vol. I, p. 524; Rypka, pp. 197–199; Browne, Vol. II, pp. 364–391.

DHU'L-RUMMA
696?–735/6?

From long line of poets; was himself a *rawi*. His poems are mostly long odes about Bedouin life, but in Arabic literature his name stands for the unrequited lover, the lover in anguish, mercilessly enslaved. Many love poems attributed to him are probably not his.
"Dhu'l Rumma," *Encyclopaedia of Islam*, 1954–, Vol. II, pp. 245–246; Blachère, Vol. III, pp. 534–536; Filshtinsky, pp. 71–73.

AL-HUTAY'A
600?–661/2?

Probably crippled or deformed, and accordingly bitter.
"Al-Hutay'a," *Encyclopaedia of Islam*, 1954–, Vol. III, p. 641; Blachère, Vol. II, pp. 327–329.

IBN HAZM
994–1064

Andalusian theologian and poet. Spent his childhood at court of Cordoba, where he received first-class education under his father's eye. After father's death (1012), various political upheavals and intrigues forced him to move from one local court to another. At times imprisoned for his politico-religious beliefs. Wrote forcefully on sectarian theological issues, and was always in the midst of theological disputes. A contemporary notes "whoever resisted him bounced off him as if off a stone." Several major works burned publicly in Seville for alleged heresies. Died near Badajos (on Spanish-Portuguese border.)

"Ibn Hazm," *Encyclopaedia of Islam*, 1954–, Vol. III, pp. 790–799; *Shorter Encyclopaedia of Islam*, pp. 147–149; Gibb, pp. 114–115. See also A. R. Nykl, *Hispano-Arabic Poetry*, Baltimore, 1946. Ibn Hazm's *al-tawq al-hamamat*, "The dove's neckring" or similar titles, has been translated into English by A. R. Nykl (Paris, 1931); into French by L. Bercher (Algiers, 1949); and into German by M. Weisweiler (Leiden, 1944); style and quality vary.

IBN AL-RUMI
836–896

Born in Baghdad of Greek ("Rumi") father and Persian mother; both probably Christian converts to Islam. Acquired reputation as poet early but about twenty became involved in Abbasid court intrigues at Baghdad and Samarra. Living in revolutionary era (Zanji rebellion, etc.), he saw suspicions, loyalties, and rewards always changing. Hence his vitriolic attacks on his contemporaries, rather like those of Martial and Juvenal. Died in poverty having tasted luxury—a skeptic. Some say he was poisoned. His imagery is precise and brilliant, greatly admired by modern Arabs. The poetry has intrinsic merit, not merely historical interest. Not to be confused with Jalal al-din Rumi, Persian mystic poet (1207–1273).

"Ibn al-Rumi," *Encyclopaedia of Islam*, 1954–, Vol. III,

pp. 907–909; Gibb, pp. 85–86; see also R. Guest, *Life and Works of Ibn er-Rumi*, London, 1944 (143 pp.); Said Bustany, *Ibn er-Rumi, sa vie et son oeuvre*, Beirut, 1967 (376 pp.).

AL-IFRIQI AL-MUTAYYAM
about 975?

In this poem he lists by name those owning palaces, cellars of treasure, slaves, horses, fine clothes, and belts of gold; hence the contemporary symbols of wealth: Paul Storr, famous eighteenth-century silversmith; Nash, English architect (1752–1835); Getty and Clore: U.S. and British millionaires. Not in standard reference works.

JALAL AL-DIN RUMI
1207–73

Born in Balkh. Died in Konya, Turkey. The greatest of many Persian mystics. Was leader of a Sufi religious order. Wrote one of the strangest and longest mystical poems known, the *Mathnawi*—unique, full of anecdotes with mystic meanings. One of Nicholson's life-long tasks was the literal translation of this poem, in which abstractions, symbols, and mystical implications are almost incomprehensible. Despite this, the *Mathnawi* is important, and should be looked at from time to time over many years. Rumi also wrote nearly two thousand quatrains and other poems. No note can do him justice. He needs profound study and much reflection to understand and appreciate.
"Djalal al-din Rumi," *Encyclopaedia of Islam*, 1954–, Vol. II, pp. 393–397 (art. by Bausani); *Shorter Encyclopaedia of Islam*, pp. 83–84 (art. by Carra de Vaux); Rypka, pp. 240–242; Browne, Vol. II, pp. 517–525; R. A. Nicholson, *The Mathnawi of Jalalu'ddin Rumi*, 1925–37, (in 6 vols.).

JAMAL ISFAHANI
died 1192

Minor Persian poet.
Rypka, pp. 213–214; Browne, Vol. II, pp. 397, 540.

JAMÍL
660?–701

Born in Hijaz. Wrote mostly love poetry. Early in life fell in love with a girl whose parents refused to let her marry him. Instead they married her off to someone wealthier. Love is never comic or frivolous with him. It is the great cosmic force and passion. To love is to suffer, to sorrow and to doubt. His "love" is almost that of mystics such as al-Ghazali (d. 1111) and Donne. Jamíl intensifies all his other emotions through being sensitized by love: to love is to perceive; sentiments close to Catullus and Elizabethan madrigalists who in loving, die.
"Djamil," *Encyclopaedia of Islam*, 1954–, Vol. II, pp. 427–428; Blachère, Vol. III, pp. 653–657; Gibb, p. 45.

KEMAL KHOJANDI
died 1401?

Persian mystic from Tabriz. Pantheist. Mostly love poetry, both *eros* and *agapê*, especially on mystical love. "One Final Fling" is a reconstruction of a point of view extrapolated from the original, and not a simple translation. It tries to catch the bitter-sweet of an old man's final love.
"Kemal Khodjandi," *Encyclopaedia of Islam*, 1913–1938, Vol. II, p. 847; Rypka, pp. 262–263.

AL-KHANSA'
590?–644?

Arab poetess. Had two brothers. One killed in a tribal raid and the second, by custom, went out to avenge his death and was himself fatally wounded. Al-Khansa' refused to be consoled and one feels that she did not want to be. Most of her poems are dirges and laments for them. Her emotional sincerity and power of lamentation come through 1,300 years later. Arabs still read her for her simplicity of language and integrity. (From a technical point of view "Lament for a Brother" is one of the most successful poems in this volume.)

"Al-Khansa'," *Encyclopaedia of Islam*, 1913–1938, Vol. II, pp. 901–902; Blachère, Vol. II, pp. 290–292; Coppier, *Le Diwan d'al Hansa'*, Beyrouth, 1889; also see works by G. Gabrieli.

KUTHAIYIR
663?–723?

Umayyad poet much ridiculed for his dwarf-like figure and his extreme religious views which were exotic rather than entirely unorthodox. He was Jamîl's *rawi*. Had passionate love for 'Azza, but some say it was simulated and not genuine—only Allah knows. Many of his poems were set to music and sung.
"Kuthaiyir," *Encyclopaedia of Islam*, 1913–1938, Vol. II, pp. 1169–1170; Blachère, Vol. III, pp. 609–616.

AL-LAJJAM AL-HARRANI
about 960?

From Harran, near Urfa in modern Turkey. Under Abbasids Harran was important center for translating works on mathematics and astronomy from Greek into Arabic. Arab pride in hospitality makes this a vilely insulting poem. Not in standard reference works.

MINUCHIHRI
died 1041?

From eastern Persia. Was major poet at court of Mahmud of Ghazna (now in Afghanistan). Many of his poems are direct translations of Arabic qasidas into Persian, but even these have acquired his own style. Wrote panegyrics, poems in praise of wine, descriptions of nature, and long poems celebrating *naw-ruz* (Persian New Year). Delighted in specific detail, quotes liberally from classical Arabic poems, often imitating them, but also includes references to ancient (non-Arab) Persian traditions. Annoyed by lack of appreciation of his talents at court, he wrote a recantation of all his former poetry in which he criticizes contemporary poets; and filled the poem with lines from famous

Arab authors the court would identify. I use famous English lines to parallel this.
"Minučihri," *Encyclopaedia of Islam*, 1913–1938, Vol. III, p. 505; Rypka, pp. 176–177; Kazimirsky, *Menoutchehri . . .*, Paris, 1886 (in French); see also C. E. Bosworth, *The Ghaznavids*, Edinburgh, 1963.

MUTANABBI
915–965

Considered by many Arabs to be the greatest of their poets; intricate, complex imagery, difficult; probably the most difficult important Arab poet for a Westerner to appreciate. Attacked and killed by marauders on his return to Baghdad from Persia. Arab scholars have studied his works intensively for several centuries, and he is still widely read.
"Mutanabbi," *Encyclopaedia of Islam*, 1913–1938, Vol. III, pp. 781–784; Nicholson, pp. 304–312; Blachère, R. *Un Poète arabe du IVe siècle de l'Hégire: Abou t-Tayyib al-Motanabbi*, Paris, 1935.

MUZAHIM AL-UQAILI
about 700?

Not in standard reference works, but see monograph by F. Krenkow, *The Poetical Remains of Muzahim al-'Uqaili*, Leiden, 1920.

NIZAMI ARUDI
about 1110?

Persian prose writer from Samarqand. Wrote up anecdotes and quoted poems by contemporary and earlier poets, including Rudaki and Rashidi Samarqandi. Wrote one of the oldest known accounts of Omar Khayyam, whom he once met in Balkh, and noted him in his *Chahar Maqala* ("Four Discourses"), in the section on astronomers, not poets. "Calling the Doctor" is based on one of his anecdotes about Ibn Sina (Avicenna), the great Persian doctor, poet, philosopher, "Renaissance man." This yarn, an eleventh-century preview of the lie-detector and *gestalt* psychology, seems worth retelling.

"Nizami Arudi," *Encyclopaedia of Islam*, 1913–1938, Vol. III, pp. 938–939; Rypka, pp. 221–222; Browne, Vol. II, pp. 336–340.

RASHIDI SAMARQANDI
about 1100?

See Nizami Arudi's *Chahar Maqala*, ed. and translated by E. G. Browne, Cambridge, 1921.

RUDAKI
870?–940/1

Born near Samarqand in what is now Uzbek S.S.R. Tradition claims he was born blind. Unlikely since his images are not those of a blind man. According to some modern Russian archaeologists who claim to have found his tomb and skull, he was deliberately blinded in old age. I am skeptical, but see "New Papers on Rudaki by Tadzhik and other Soviet scholars," by J. Bečka in *Archiv Orientalni* (Prague), 28, 1960, pp. 494–501 (in English). Rudaki was prolific; early references to vast quantities of his poetry exist—mostly lost. Its simplicity went out of fashion, but in recent times his works have become better known through the scholarship of Said Nafisy (mostly in Persian). Basil Bunting's translations of Rudaki's lament in his old age, "All the teeth ever I had are worn down . . ." and of one of the quatrains, "Came to me . . . Who? . . ." are superb. Research on Rudaki using Russian sources would be valuable.

"Rudaki," *Encyclopaedia of Islam*, 1913–1938, Vol. III, pp. 1168–1169; Rypka, pp. 144–145; I. S. Braginskiy, *Rudaki Stikhi, Redaktsiya i Kommentariy*, Nauka Publishing House, Moscow, 1964 (in Russian); B. Bunting, *Collected Poems*, Fulcrum Press, London, 1968, pp. 141–144.

AL-TIRIMMAH
660?–725?

Born in Syria-Palestine. Involved in several political religious movements as a propagandist. Traveled extensively in Persia and Iraq. He was deeply involved in spread of Islam, possibly as a soldier, and the religious sentiment in some of his poems is that of the crusader, eager and willing to die for his faith. "Lord of the Throne," one of his best-known poems, combines his pious vigor and desert realism. "In the Heart of the Desert" portrays in three lines a man laughing at himself, a true humanist sentiment. This poem is still with us now. Classical scholars in Baghdad claimed al-Tirimmah used obscure and rare words. They therefore preserved his fragments by quoting him frequently. Modern scholars believe these rare words came from his youthful contacts with isolated Bedouin tribes.

"Al-Tirimmah," *Encyclopaedia of Islam*, 1913–1938, Vol. IV, p. 794; Blachère, Vol. III, pp. 530–534; F. Krenkow, *The Poems of Tufail ibn 'Auf al-Ghanawi and at-Tirimmah ibn Hakim at-Ta'yi*, London, 1927.

Bibliographical Note

Basic reference works are *Encyclopaedia of Islam*, 4 vols. and *Supplement*, 1913–1938; *Encyclopaedia of Islam, New Edition*, 1954–, 2 vols. completed, and Vol. III in progress; Sauvaget's *Introduction to the History of the Muslim East, A Bibliographical Guide based on the second edition as recast by Claude Cahen*, University of California Press, 1965; and J. D. Pearson's *Index Islamicus*, 1906–1955, *Supplement*, 1956–1960, *Second Supplement*, 1961–1965. Clues for tracking down nearly all monographs on authors writing in Arabic and Persian are to be found in these three works. Bibliographical information will be found at end of articles in each edition of the *Encyclopaedia of Islam*. The *Encyclopaedia of Islam* is awkward to use sometimes, and the transliteration is confusing. Sauvaget's *Introduction* is essential. It is a long bibliographical essay, well organized and well written, but rather overwhelming. Pearson indexes a wide range of articles from scholarly journals. Substantial supplements listing 7,000–8,000 new articles appear every five years. Note in particular East European journals. Some are exceptionally important, and articles often have summaries in French, English, or Russian. Note also, printed catalogue of the library of the London School of Oriental and African Studies in twenty-eight volumes (not all Islamic); plus First Supplement, 16 vols., 1968. Author index is excellent, but subject index poor.

For pre-Islamic poetry, see works by Sir Charles Lyall; for Arabic poetry in Spain, see works by Nykl, Henri Pérès, Levi-Provençal, and S. M. Stern. Other works are listed in Sauvaget's *Introduction*. Note also journal, *Al-Andalus*, and recent work by Salah Khalis, *La Vie Littéraire à Seville au XIe Siècle*, Editions Nationales Algériennes, SNED, Alger, 1966. On traditions of courtly love in Arabic, see J.-C. Vadet, *L'Esprit Courtois en Orient, dans les cinqs premiers siècles de l'Hégire*, Paris, 1968.

For general cultural history, see Brockelmann, *History of the*

Islamic Peoples, London, 1949 (very compact, difficult, but essential); P. K. Hitti, *History of the Arabs*, various editions (readable, with emphasis on cultural history); B. Spuler, *The Muslim World, A Historical Survey*, in three parts, translated from the German by F. R. C. Bagley, 1960–1969 (an excellent survey, good maps, fairly readable, recommended highly); Henri Terrasse, *Islam d'Espagne*, Librairie Plon, Paris, 1958 (with particular emphasis on architecture). For those wishing to see their history, Hazard's *Atlas of Islamic History*, Princeton University Press, 1954, and Roolvink's *Historical Atlas of the Muslim Peoples*, Amsterdam, 1957, are excellent, scholarly, fascinating publications. Hazard's historical notes are brilliantly concise.

General surveys of Arabic literature: H. A. R. Gibb, *Arabic Literature*, 2nd rev. ed., Oxford, 1963 (includes useful bibliography of translations); R. A. Nicholson, *A Literary History of the Arabs*, 1907 (important but some details out of date); R. Blachère, *Histoire de la Littérature Arabe*, 3 vols. to date, 1954, 1964, 1966 (in progress, monumental to date, excellent bibliographies after each main entry). Other works by Nallino, Gabrieli, Abd al-Jalil, Pellat, and Wiet are all useful. Filshtinsky's *Arabic Literature*, Nauka Publishing House, Moscow, 1966, translated from Russian, hardly known in the West, is best cheap paperback survey (234 pp.). It includes generous quotes from Arab poets, many in antiquated English, but no worse than Nicholson's Edwardian style. Kritzeck's *Anthology of Islamic Literature*, Pelican, 1964, includes prose and poetry. For catalogues of Arabic manuscripts, see Brockelmann, and Sezgin.

For Persian literature, see E. G. Browne, *A Literary History of Persia*, 4 vols., 1902–1924 (Invaluable compilation but out of date, translations are accurate but archaic. Vols. I and II superior to III and IV). Jan Rypka's *A History of Iranian Literature*, Dordrecht, 1968, differs in structure from Browne, less encyclopaedic, but more penetrating. Likely to remain standard work for many years. Includes superb but discouraging bibliography.

To understand something of Persian criteria for judging their own poetry, read sections: National Individuality, pp. 76–85; Conservatism and Convention in Persian Literature, pp. 87–90; Poetry and its Forms, pp. 91–108. With Rypka now available in English, the previously useful survey by Arberry is now insignificant. Reuben Levy's posthumous *Introduction to Persian Literature*, Columbia University Press, 1969, is adequate, but pedestrian. It lacks Rypka's insight. Levy's earlier survey, *Persian Literature*, 1923, is out of date and misleading. Russian works by Bertels, Braginskiy, and others listed in Rypka are important, but mostly untranslated. On the earliest poetry, see G. Lazard, *Les premiers poètes persans*, Paris, 1964. Massé's *Anthologie Persane*, Payot, Paris, 1950, is mediocre. Much better is Z. Safâ's *Anthologie de la poésie persane*, Gallimard, Paris, 1964. Most English translations from Persian are bad English verse, but many small volumes exist. For Arabic/Persian influences, see Daudpota, *The influence of Arabic poetry on the development of Persian poetry*, Bombay, 1934, also relevant sections in Rypka. For catalogue of Persian manuscripts, see C. A. Storey.